Aviation

Cool Women
Who Fly

GIRLS
IN
SCIENCE

Carmella Van Vleet

Illustrated by
Lena Chandhok

Nomad Press
A division of Nomad Communications
10 9 8 7 6 5 4 3 2 1

This book was manufactured by CGB Printers,
North Mankato, Minnesota, United States
September 2016, Job #208068

ISBN Softcover: 978-1-61930-440-6
ISBN Hardcover: 978-1-61930-436-9

Educational Consultant, Marla Conn
Cover Photo Credit: © Larry Grace Photography

Questions regarding the ordering of this book should be addressed to
Nomad Press
2456 Christian St.
White River Junction, VT 05001
www.nomadpress.net

Printed in the United States.

~ Titles in the **Girls in Science** Series ~

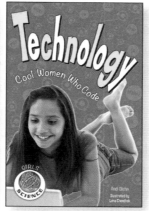

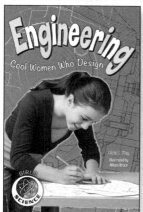

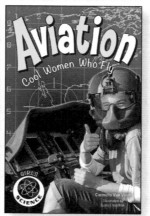

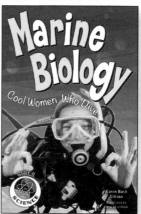

Check out more titles at www.nomadpress.net

How to Use This Book

In this book you'll find a few different ways to explore the topic of women in aviation.

The essential questions in each Ask & Answer box encourage you to think further. You probably won't find the answers to these questions in the text, and sometimes there are no right or wrong answers! Instead, these questions are here to help you think more deeply about what you're reading and how the material connects to your own life.

There's a lot of new vocabulary in this book! Can you figure out a word's meaning from the paragraph? Look in the glossary in the back of the book to find the definitions of words you don't know.

Are you interested in what women have to say about aviation? You'll find quotes from women who are professionals in the aviation field. You can learn a lot by listening to people who have worked hard to succeed!

Primary sources come from people who were eyewitnesses to events. They might write about the event, take pictures, or record the event for radio or video. Why are primary sources important?

PS Interested in primary sources? Look for this icon.

Use a QR code reader app on your tablet or other device to find online primary sources. You can find a list of URLs on the Resources page. If the QR code doesn't work, try searching the Internet with the Keyword Prompts to find other helpful sources.

CONTENTS

aerial
aviation
aviatrix
aeronautics
buoyancy
discipline
airfoil
aircraft
hanger
blimp
ballistic
glider
roll
pilot
aerospace
simulator
pitch
navigator
bush pilot
Flyer
dirigible
airship
rudder
motivation
engineer
altitude
laser
radar
yaw
drone
base
jetliner
technology
journalist
apprentice
combat
aviator
radio wave
maneuverable
sexism
cabin crew
homeschool
afterburner
labyrinth
vessel
codex
Mach
troops
internship
aeronautical engineer
ground instructor
ornithopter
flight engineer
air show
biplane
toxic
thrust
turbulence
solo
call sign
stealth technology
sonic boom
hydrogen gas
turbine
brief
debrief
atmosphere
pressure
goods
zeppelin
FAA
cambered wing
inhospitable
bi-wing
certified flight instructor
commercial pilot's license
meteorology
protagonist
production support engineer
supercruise
cataract
mythology
steam engine
discrimination
blockade
modification
perpendicular

INTRODUCTION
Up and Away!

When you look up into the sky and see an airplane, you might wonder where it's going. But have you ever wondered who's flying it? And how did they become a pilot? Perhaps you've taken a trip and flown on a plane. How does such a heavy machine manage to get off the ground in the first place? Who was the first person to imagine this was possible?

We use airplanes and other aircraft for all kinds of things—to travel, to protect ourselves, and to move goods across great distances. We even use them to study weather and traffic patterns.

An aircraft is a vehicle that uses air and buoyancy to fly. Any activity that has to do with the design, development, production, and operation of aircraft is called aviation. A person who operates, or pilots, an aircraft is called an aviator.

The Myth of Daedalus

One of the earliest stories about flight comes from Greek mythology. Daedalus was a man who built a great labyrinth, or maze, for King Minos of Crete. The king imprisoned Daedalus and his son, Icarus, in the center of the labyrinth because Daedalus betrayed the king. But Daedalus and Icarus made wings out of tree branches and wax and escaped. Unfortunately, Icarus was young and too enthusiastic about flying. Even though his father warned him, he flew too close to the sun and the wax in the wings melted. He fell into the sea and drowned. Some cultures interpret this story as meaning, "Pride comes before a fall."

There are many different jobs you can do in aviation. Of course, one is working as a pilot. But there are many other roles that need to be filled, too.

In *Aviation: Cool Women Who Fly*, you'll read about the history of aviation. You'll also meet three women who are working in this fascinating field. Meg Godlewski is a master certified flight instructor (MCFI) who loves teaching others how to fly. Taylor McConnell has a degree in aeronautical engineering technology and is starting her career as a production support engineer. Kristin Wolfe got her degree in chemical engineering and then joined the Air Force. She now flies the F-22 Raptor, a stealth tactical military plane.

These women faced many obstacles along the way and worked hard to achieve their goals. They demonstrated that you don't need actual wings to soar. Before we meet them, let's learn about the interesting history of aviation and how humans learned to fly!

66 Aviation, this young modern giant, exemplifies the possible relationship of women with the creations of science. 99

—Amelia Earhart,
aviator

CHAPTER 1

Into the Wild, Blue Yonder

If someone asked you what superpower you'd most like to have, would you say the ability to fly? Many people would! Since the beginning of time, people have dreamed of taking to the skies. In ancient times, people thought flying was as simple as flapping wings. Many built their own versions of wings and jumped from high places. Of course, this often ended with terrible results.

Maybe there was something more to how birds' wings worked than just flapping them up and down. This was what Leonardo da Vinci believed. Da Vinci was an Italian artist, mathematician, and scientist who lived more than 500 years ago, from 1452 to 1519. After studying birds in flight, he drew sketches of machines with flapping wings called ornithopters.

As far as we know, da Vinci never built any of his machines. They probably would have been too heavy to work. But his ideas helped increase our understanding about flight.

In the late 1700s, people began experimenting with hot air balloons. Because hot air is less dense than cold air, it rises. People also used hydrogen gas to lift balloons because it is less dense than air.

(PS)

Leonardo da Vinci's Work

Da Vinci collected his sketches and ideas about topics into notebooks called codices. Do you have a journal? What kind of things do you keep in it? You can peek into da Vinci's codex on flight by watching this video from the Smithsonian National Air and Space Museum.

air space da Vinci codex 🔍

Hot air balloons gave balloonists and their passengers a taste of flying. But there was a problem. Balloons couldn't be easily steered. In the 1850s, people solved this by adding steam engines and rudders. Rudders are vertical blades used to change directions on a vessel. The results were airships, also called dirigibles.

There are two kinds of dirigibles—zeppelins and blimps. Zeppelins are airships that have rigid frames, while blimps have no rigid structure and inflate like balloons.

By the 1920s, dirigibles were quite popular. But after multiple accidents, it was clear they weren't the answer to our desire to fly. Today, we still use dirigibles, but they are a smaller part of aviation. And they are much safer than they used to be!

Ask & Answer

Why do you think early aviators kept trying to fly even though their work was often dangerous?

The Hindenburg

The 1937 Hindenburg disaster is a famous zeppelin accident. The aircraft left Frankfurt, Germany, and crossed the Atlantic Ocean. It was attempting to land in Lakehurst, New Jersey, when the zeppelin exploded. Thirty-six people were killed.

In 1937, you couldn't just turn on your television to watch events. You had to listen to the radio to get live accounts. The radio broadcast of the Hindenburg disaster as described by reporter Herbert Morrison is considered to be one of the most famous radio broadcasts ever. You can watch a composite, or mix, of the news video and the radio broadcast here.

Hindenburg disaster with sound archives 🔍

GLIDING INTO FLIGHT

Having you ever flown a kite and watched how it dipped and bobbed and floated on the air currents? Early aviators did that, too. Inspired by kites, Sir George Cayley (1773–1857) from Britain began experimenting with gliders.

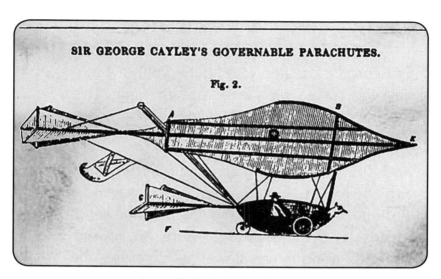

photo credit: *Mechanics' Magazine*, 1852

Gliders are aircraft without engines. They float, or glide, on air currents after being launched. In a way, Sir George was the first aeronautical engineer. An aeronautical engineer is someone who figures out how to make all the parts of an aircraft work together.

Early gliders looked similar to what we now call hang gliders. They didn't always fly well, though. Like early air balloons, they were difficult to control. But later, in the 1890s, a German man named Otto Lilienthal (1848–1896) improved the glider's design. He figured out how to make them more reliable. Because of his work, Otto is often called "the world's first true aviator." His work also earned him the nickname "Flying Man."

HOW WINGS WORK

Sir George is credited with figuring out that an unevenly curved wing works best for flight. This is called a cambered wing. How do the wings on an aircraft work?

Air is like water—it flows around objects. As an airplane moves along the ground, air travels over and under its wings. Air moving over the wing speeds up, creating lower pressure. Air flowing under the wing moves slower, which causes the pressure to increase and push up. This is how a plane is lifted off the ground.

Explore!

See wings in action in your own backyard! Research a variety of ways to fold paper planes. Next, create several planes and test them. Which design flies the farthest? Do you think the kind of paper you use affects how well the plane flies? What else might affect the distance a paper plane flies?

Here's a good site for ideas.

paper airplanes HQ 🔍

Different types of wings have different shapes. The shape of a wing is called an airfoil, but people also refer to the wing itself as an airfoil. Other objects used to lift or control aircraft, such as propellers or rudders, can also be called airfoils.

THE WRIGHT STUFF

In Dayton, Ohio, two brothers were also working on making flight a reality. Orville and Wilber Wright were followers of Sir George Cayley's and Otto Lilienthal's work, and they were determined to build and fly the world's first airplane.

Orville (1871–1948) and his older brother, Wilber (1867–1912), built and repaired bicycles for a living. Their parents, especially their mother, Susan Wright, encouraged them to explore and try new things.

Susan Wright was an educated woman, which was unusual at the time. She grew up helping her father in his repair shop. Susan taught Orville and Wilber to fix objects around the house and to make things.

66 We were lucky enough to grow up in an environment where there was always encouragement to children to pursue intellectual interests, to investigate whatever aroused curiosity. 99

—Orville Wright

Like many before them, the Wright brothers realized that the biggest challenge in flight was controlling the aircraft. They built and tested many gliders and decided that a bi-wing design would work best. Eventually, they built a plane with an engine they named *Flyer*.

The brothers tested *Flyer* out in the windy, spacious, sandy area of Kitty Hawk, North Carolina. On December 17, 1903, with Orville acting as pilot, *Flyer* flew for 12 seconds and went 120 feet!

Like their mother, Orville and Wilber's sister, Katharine, supported their work even as she established a successful teaching career. Not only did she take care of the family after their mother died, she also handled the brothers' business. This included their bicycle shop and their flying machines.

Ask & Answer

The early planes were made of wood. Today, we usually use a metal called aluminum. Why do you think that is?

The *Flyer*

Flyer made four successful flights on December 17, 1903. One of the Wright brothers' helpers, John Daniels, caught the first one on camera. You can see the footage here.

NASA video first Wright flight 🔍

Katharine was the only one of the Wright children to earn a college degree. She was sometimes called the "Third Wright Brother" and was given the French Legion of Honor medal.

The Wright brothers, as well as other early aviators, were famous. They were like rocks stars of the time! As early aviators learned more and more about the science behind flight, people gathered from all over to watch. Air shows became popular events.

WOMEN TAKE TO THE SKY

In the early days of aviation, many people believed that women wouldn't make good pilots. They thought women weren't brave or physically strong enough to fly. After all, aviation was new and still dangerous.

But plenty of women were just as eager and skilled as men when it came to piloting. And these female aviators, often called aviatrixes, made significant contributions to the field.

Have you ever been to an air show? These are exciting demonstrations of aircraft and piloting skills. A French woman named Elise Raymonde de Laroche (1882–1919) went to one in 1908. An accomplished balloonist, she couldn't pass up the chance to fly with Wilber Wright when he offered a free ride to any woman who was in the crowd!

Elise was so inspired by this flying experience that she quit her job as an actress and became the first female pilot in 1910. She later flew and competed with men in air shows.

Elise Raymonde de Laroche,
the first woman to receive an airline pilot's license

In June 1919, Elise set a women's altitude record. Unfortunately, she was killed later that same week when the plane she was riding aboard crashed.

An American named Harriet Quimby (1875–1912) was another woman inspired by air shows. A journalist and screenwriter, she longed for more excitement.

Other Pioneer Aviatrixes

Here a few of the other women who pioneered aviation.

- Bessie "Queen Bess" Coleman (1892–1926) was the first African American woman to get her pilot's license.

- Geraldine "Jerrie" Mock (1925–2014) was the first woman to complete the round-the-world trip that Amelia Earhart was attempting when she disappeared.

- Katherine Cheung (1904–2003) was the first Asian American woman to get a pilot's license.

- Willa Brown (1906–1992) was the first African American woman to earn both a private and commercial pilot's license.

- Helen Richey (1909–1947) was the first female captain of a commercial airline.

Read about these aviators here.

WAI notable women aviation history 🔍

> 66 The men flyers have given out the impression that aeroplaning is very perilous work . . . but when I saw how easily man flyers manipulated their machines I said I could fly. 99
>
> **—Harriet Quimby,**
> aviator

In 1911, Harriet became the first American female pilot. She became the first woman to fly at night. A year later, Harriet was the first woman to fly solo over the English Channel. This is the stretch of water between Great Britain and Europe. Like Elise Raymonde de Laroche, Harriet was killed in an airplane crash.

As the field of aviation grew, it sparked the imaginations and competitiveness of pilots. Prizes were offered to people who were the first to do something or break a flying distance record. Charles Lindberg became one of these pilots.

Aboard his plane, *The Spirit of St. Louis,* Charles was the first person to fly from New York to Paris. This flight later inspired one of the most famous pilots of all time—Amelia Earhart.

Amelia was a record-setting, charismatic pilot and author. She went around the country sharing her passion for flying. Her disappearance during her final flight over the Pacific Ocean is a great mystery that continues to intrigue people today.

MODERN TIMES

Planes proved to be very useful during World War I and World War II. For the first time, soldiers could get a good look at the ground and see where the enemy troops were. Following the wars, airplanes continued to become more efficient and safer. In 1938, the Boeing 247 was introduced. This was the first modern passenger airplane.

Women in Aviation Groups

There are many organizations that encourage and help girls and women who are interested in aviation. Here is a list of several of these organizations. To learn more, do an Internet search of the name of the group.

- Women in Aviation International
- The Ninety-Nines Inc.
- Whirly Girls
- Association for Women in Aviation Maintenance
- The International Society of Women Airline Pilots
- Girls with Wings

Have you ever taken a trip on an airplane? Was it special? Maybe you dressed up or maybe you just wore your most comfortable clothes and shoes.

In the early days of commercial flight, flying was a big deal. It was considered glamorous and people often dressed in their best clothes. Airports were not glamorous, though. Many times, they were little more than a dirt road in the middle of a field!

In the 1950s, jetliners became popular. These are airplanes powered by one or more jet engines. They can hold a large number of people, making it possible for even more people to travel by air.

Amelia Earhart

Amelia Earhart (1897–disappeared 1937) was born in Atchison, Kansas. She had a difficult childhood and moved often, but she loved to read and learn. During World War I, she worked as a nurse's aide. One day, she and her sister went to an air show where pilots were doing stunts. She found it thrilling.

Shortly afterward, Amelia began flying lessons. In 1923, she became the 16th woman to earn an international pilot's license. She quickly began setting distance and altitude records. Her most famous one was being the first woman to fly solo across the Atlantic Ocean.

Amelia Earhart,
the first woman to fly solo across the Atlantic Ocean

photo credit: *Los Angeles Daily News*

Amelia wrote books and did public appearances about her work. She inspired many other women to go into the field of aviation.

In 1937, while attempting to fly around the world, Amelia and her navigator, Fred Noonan, disappeared over the Pacific Ocean. Her plane was never found and her disappearance continues to be one of the greatest aviation mysteries. She was declared legally dead in 1939.

You can see a timeline of Amelia's life here. What do you think happened to Amelia and her plane?

PBS timeline Earhart 🔍

The view from the pilot's seat
is much more complicated than it used to be.

Today's planes are highly advanced. They have technology designed to do everything from fly the plane without a pilot, hide from enemy radar, observe the weather, and connect to the Internet. Modern planes are quieter, go faster, and carry more people than the planes of the past. All of this makes flying one of the fastest and safest ways to travel.

Airplanes and other aircraft need more than just the pilots and other cabin crew members, though. There are many jobs in aviation.

Do you like to fix things and work on puzzles? Maybe you'd be a good aircraft mechanic, which is someone who works on engines or the plane itself. Maybe you could be a production support engineer, which is someone who takes care of any problems a new plane might have before it's sold.

Maybe you like to design new things. You could be an aeronautical engineer. If you like to help people, you could be a helicopter pilot and fly sick and injured people to hospitals. Maybe you'd like to use planes to protect your country as a member of the military.

Technology in aviation is quickly expanding. For instance, drones, or unmanned aerial vehicles, are growing in popularity. They can be used to do everything from deliver goods, film movies, and keep an eye on enemies or dangerous situations. Drones don't fly themselves, and they need skilled pilots to control them from the ground.

Ask & Answer

Which would make you want to try something new and challenging: having someone tell you that you *can* do something or someone telling you that you *can't* do something? Why?

As you can see, aviation is an exciting field with lots of opportunities! Even so, it's still a field mostly populated by men.

Gender discrimination is when someone thinks a person can't do a good job because of their gender. Historically, women have been subject to unfair gender discrimination and have been prevented from getting jobs in the fields they want to work in. This is changing as women receive the same opportunities as men.

According to the Federal Aviation Administration (FAA), in 2013, women made up a little more than 6 percent of pilots and just less than 4 percent of the flight engineers in the United States. Some studies say one of the reasons women don't go into aviation as often as men is because they have fewer role models. Girls and women especially need people who encourage them.

Whether you are thinking about going into aviation or are simply interested in learning more, there's exciting information in this book. You'll read about Meg Godlewski, Taylor McConnell, and Kristen Wolfe, three women who dreamed of flying as young girls. They have worked hard to go into aviation. Maybe their stories will inspire your own dreams to soar!

CHAPTER 2

Meg Godlewski

If you came across Meg Godlewski on the runway or in the classroom on the right day, you might find her leaning over and cutting the shirttail off someone's shirt. Don't worry! She's just continuing a tradition of flying instructors. In this tradition, an instructor cuts the shirttail of a student who's just taken their first solo flight. Meg teaches people how to fly airplanes.

Meg was born on June 18, 1968, near Sunnyvale, California. Her parents, George and Kay, had three daughters. Meg is the middle child.

Meg's mom was a psychologist. This is someone who studies the mind and people's behavior. Her dad was an aerospace engineer for an aerospace company called Lockheed. An engineer is someone who designs, builds, or maintains things. An aerospace company is one that designs and builds aircraft and other flying machines, such as spacecraft. Meg and her family lived near Moffett Federal Airfield.

Jeana Yeager

When Jeana Yeager (1952–) was a young girl, she was interested in helicopters. As an adult, she worked as a draftswoman for an energy company. A draftswoman is someone who draws technical plans. Later, she worked at an aerospace company. Her interest in flying continued, and she earned her private pilot's license at age 26.

Jeana intended to learn to fly helicopters, but soon became interested in high-performance and experimental aircraft instead. One day at lunch, Jeana and fellow pilot Dick Rutan, along with his brother, Burt, who was an aircraft designer, talked about building a plane to break the distance record. Jeana helped raised the $2 million they needed.

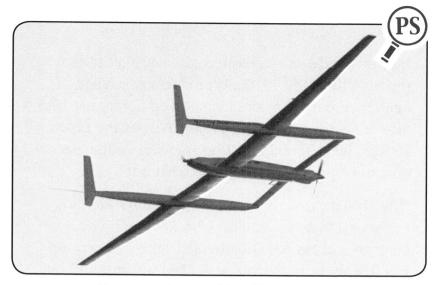

Voyager on its record-breaking, nonstop, unrefueled flight around the world

photo credit: NASA

She also helped design the aircraft, *Voyager*, which had modifications for the challenge. From idea to test flight, the project took five years!

On December 14, 1986, Jeana and her copilot, Dick, took off from Edwards Air Force base in California. They became the first aviators to fly around the globe without stopping to refuel. It took 9 days, 13 minutes, and 44 seconds.

The trip was very difficult. They had to deal with exhaustion and tight quarters. Loud engines left Jeana with hearing damage. But thousands of people watched and cheered as the *Voyager*, Jeana, and Dick landed in the history books on December 23, 1986, back at Edwards Air Force base.

Moffett Field was established as a naval air station (NAS) in the early 1930s. It's in Mountain View, California, but it was originally called Sunnyvale NAS after a nearby town. Sunnyvale NAS was the base for U.S. Navy dirigibles. Who wants to imagine a dirigible flying into a mountain? No one!

"My parents took me to the Moffett NAS Air Show every year," Meg says. Like Elise Raymonde de Laroche and Harriet Quimby and other women we learned about in chapter one, Meg was inspired by the planes and daring pilots. Her parents supported her passion.

The fighter-bomber Lockheed P-38 Lightning, 1943
photo credit: U.S. Air Force

"[My] mom bought me a model P-38 Lightning because it was her favorite airplane when she was a teen growing up during WWII," Meg shares. The P-38 Lightning was a fighter plane. "[My] dad used to bring home photos of Lockheed projects. When I was seven, I recreated the cockpit of the Lockheed space plane in a cardboard box in my bedroom."

Meg says family and friends recall her as being "fearless" as a young girl. She also had an active imagination. Sometimes, she climbed on top of her backyard fort and pretended she was flying World War II bombing missions. She used her stuffed animals to act as her crew.

Meg re-enacted the Berlin Airlift. This was a mission by the United States and the United Kingdom to bring food and other supplies to parts of Berlin, Germany, that were blockaded by the Soviet Union. Meg threw candy to her friends below! Another time, she built her own working hang glider using a tube tent, a backpack, and bungee cords. "It was unstable, but it flew," she says.

66 The women pilots were paid less than their male counterparts. . . . At least we were eventually allowed to wear trousers with our uniforms. 99

—Diana Barnato Walker,
pilot during World War II

At school, Meg loved science and history. The variety of sports she participated in included volleyball, field hockey, softball, soccer, and track and field. She played multiple instruments and wrote songs.

Meg also loved to write. "I wrote lots of fiction in junior high and high school . . . most of my fiction was action-adventure because there were no real action-adventure stories with girls as the protagonists," Meg says. In high school she joined the school newspaper and thought about becoming a journalist someday. A journalist is someone who writes for a newspaper or magazine. Journalists also prepare news for broadcast on television or the Internet.

When she grew up, Meg wanted to be a pilot, too. But when she was 12, she got glasses. She doesn't remember who it was, but someone told her she couldn't be a pilot if she had glasses. "It was something I always wanted to do," Meg says. "But because I have corrected vision, I thought aviation wasn't open to me. It wasn't until I got out of college that I realized aviation was an option."

Ask & Answer

Has anyone ever told you that you can't do something just because you're a girl or a boy or because you have a physical limitation? How did that make you feel?

Berlin Airlift:
The Berlin Candy Bomber

During World War II (1939–1945), the United States and its allies dropped food and other supplies into Berlin, Germany. This operation was called the Berlin Airlift. U.S. World War II pilot Lt. Gail Halvorsen was one of the soldiers who helped on this mission. One day, he decided to drop candy from his airplane for the children. He used handkerchiefs as parachutes! As you can imagine, the children loved this. They called Gail the "Berlin Candy Bomber" and the "Chocolate Bomber" and "Uncle Wiggly Wings." He got this last nickname because he'd wiggle the wings of his plane so the kids would know when he was overhead.

Gail used handkerchiefs and other bits of material to make miniature parachutes for the candy. Experiment with different designs and materials and see if you can come up with a way to safely drop an unboiled egg from five feet off the ground!

You can hear Gail talk about how he got the idea here.

wiggly wings 🔍

photo credit: The Harry S. Truman Library and Museum

THE YOUNG PILOT

After high school, Meg attended Humboldt State University in California and got a degree in journalism/public relations. She got into radio broadcasting and even had her own college show playing old rock and roll music. She also learned the art of sound engineering and audio production. All of these skills would prove useful later on. "I was never afraid of the radio when I became a pilot," Meg says.

The radio station Meg worked for ran ads for a local flight school. After she graduated, the station gave her an introductory flight lesson as a gift.

Meg was hooked! Once she realized it didn't matter that she wore glasses or that she was a girl, she was determined to earn her pilot's license.

But flight lessons are expensive. It can cost between $6,000 and $9,000 to get your pilot's license. And the price can go up depending on different things, such as the cost of fuel and what kind of aircraft you're training in.

Ask & Answer

It can take a long time to become a pilot. Many people give up along the way. Have you ever done anything that took a long time to achieve? What made you stick with it?

Like many people learning to fly, Meg had to work hard to pay for air time. She spent five years at various jobs. She worked at a newspaper and took part-time side jobs, such as a store clerk, just to scrape together enough money to keep taking flying lessons. She even anchored sports at a television station. But she hated being on camera.

Getting a pilot's license can take a long time. You have to fly, or log, a minimum of 40 hours to become a private pilot. A private pilot is someone who is allowed to fly an airplane and carry passengers, but cannot fly in all weather conditions or get paid to fly.

In order to transport paying passengers or goods, you must have a commercial pilot's license. You need between 170 and 250 hours of flight experience to earn a commercial license.

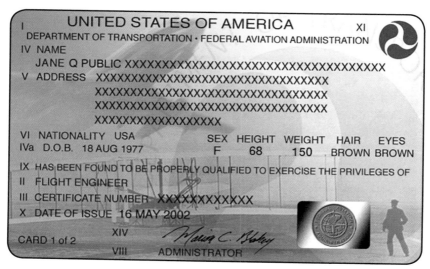

Front side of a U.S. pilot's certificate, issued by the FAA

After Meg earned her pilot's license, she began writing articles for a newspaper called *General Aviation News*. Her editors wanted her to take the instrument rating test so she could use the company airplane.

Passing this test means that you've undergone intensive training on instruments. You are allowed to fly in clouds and other weather conditions where you have to rely on your cockpit instruments instead of sight alone.

When a pilot can't see because of the weather conditions, she or he must rely on their instrument panel. Tools such as radar can tell a pilot where their plane is in relationship to the ground and other distant objects. Radar is a device that uses radio waves to produce images.

Ask & Answer

Meg thought getting her commercial pilot's license would give her more authority when she wrote about aviation. Do you think people who write about things should be able do them? Can you be an expert on something without experiencing it?

Jessica Cox

Jessica Cox was born in 1983. She was born without arms, but has not let that challenge hold her back. She uses her feet to do things other people use their hands for, such as drive a car, use a computer, write, and eat. After three years of training, at age 25, Jessica became the world's first armless licensed pilot. "I didn't see my not having arms as a limitation," she said in an interview.

You can watch a short video about Jessica and her achievements at this website.

Jessica Cox limb-itless 🔍

Flying without being able to see everything around you might not sound like a good idea. But what would happen if pilots could never fly in cloudy weather? We'd probably never be able to get anywhere in a timely or safe fashion.

After Meg got her private pilot's license, she decided to pursue her commercial pilot's license. She thought it might give her more authority when she wrote about aviation. Plus, with a commercial license she could work as a pilot for individuals or companies.

While she was still earning her certificate, her instructor suddenly quit. It turned out that he was only teaching so he could become a pilot for a commercial airline. Meg hired a new instructor, but his goal was to leave teaching and become an airline pilot, too.

"I fired him and decided I would pursue my instructor's certificate, because I didn't want to be an airline pilot," Meg says. "I would be the instructor who stayed."

Ellen Evak Paneok

In some places around the world, pilots fly in extreme conditions. Pilots who fly in remote and inhospitable areas are called bush pilots. They frequently deal with conditions such as high winds, freezing temperatures, and snowy landing strips.

Bush pilots are vital to the scientists who work in extreme environments, such as the South Pole. Because there are no stores or hospitals at the bottom of the world, people rely on pilots to deliver supplies and evacuate the sick or injured.

Alaska is another place with challenging conditions. Only about 10 percent of Alaska is accessible by roads! Air travel is the state's main mode of transportation. About 1 percent of Alaska's population are pilots. Most of these 7,500 pilots are men. But there are female bush pilots, too.

> 66 When I began to talk about flying, she already had confidence in me. My mother never warned me not to do this or that for fear of being hurt. Of course I got hurt, but I was never afraid. 99

—Katherine Stinson,
fourth American woman
to earn her pilot's license

Ellen Evak Paneok was one.

Ellen (1959–2008) was an artist, writer, and Alaska's first Native American female bush pilot. She came from Inupiat ancestry. Ellen was inspired to learn how to fly after reading an article about aviation as a teenager. By the time she was just 23, she'd earned both her private and commercial pilot's licenses. She flew passengers, medical patients, and cargo that included mail, animals, and even dynamite! In 2012, she was inducted into the Alaskan Women's Hall of Fame. She is one of the 37 pilots featured in the "Women and Flight" exhibit at the Smithsonian museum in Washington, D.C.

Learn more about Ellen and hear her interviewed at this website.

Ellen Evak Paneok
Project Jukebox 🔍

TEACHING OTHERS

On July 23, 2003, Meg got her instructor's certificate, making her a certified flight instructor. She's been teaching ever since.

Exactly two years later, in 2005, she was named a master instructor by the National Association of Flight Instructors (NAFI). In 2007, Meg also earned the FAA Gold Seal, which is a recognition for flight instructors who have a good pass rate for first-time students. That same year, she was also recognized as a master instructor of flight and master ground instructor by the Society of Aviation and Flight Educators (SAFE).

A ground instructor teaches people what they need to know to pass the written part of their pilot's test. To earn these titles, which are recognized by the FAA, an instructor must demonstrate a commitment to excellence and professional growth as well as serve the aviation community in positive ways. They must also pass a review from their peers. NAFI has four areas in which pilots must qualify, while SAFE has five.

Ask & Answer

What traits do you think a good teacher has? Do you think you'd be a good teacher?

Controlling an Airplane

Flying an airplane is not like driving a car. A car can go left or right, backward or forward. But an airplane moves in three dimensions, or areas of space. A plane's nose can move up, or climb. And it can move down, or dive. This is called "pitch." The wings can "roll," or tip, from side to side. A plane's control column controls both its pitch and roll. A plane can also "yaw" or move from left to right. The rudder controls yaw.

To fly a plane, a pilot often has to control the pitch, roll, and yaw, all at the same time. This requires them to move both of their feet and both of their hands, sometimes in different directions. You have to be very coordinated!

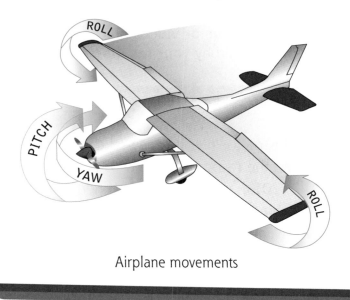

Airplane movements

Log Your Homework Hours

Pilots often use the word "log" to describe flying time. For example, they might say, "I logged four hours today." Have you ever wondered why they say this?

Pilots have to follow rules when they fly. This means letting airports know when they're taking off and landing and where they are in the air. It also means keeping track of the dates and times they fly. They put this information into logbooks.

Have you ever kept track of your activities? Start your own logbook. Keep track of when you do certain things and how long you spend on them. How much time do you spend on homework? How much time do you spend watching television or videos on the Internet? Are you surprised by your results?

The master instructor title is renewed every two years. Meg received the recognition from SAFE again in 2009, 2011, 2013, and 2015, making her one of 23 instructors from around the world to earn the master credentials five times! She is currently one of only 22 instructors in the world to be a master of ground instruction and a master of flight instruction at the same time.

A typical day of teaching for Meg starts with preparations. She needs to do many things before actually taking a student into the air for a lesson. For example, when she first arrives at the airport, she must make sure the airplane is properly fueled and that the windshield is clean and the oil level in the engine is good.

She needs to figure out the best flight routes for each student to take so she can make sure they're learning all they can. She also needs to check the weather throughout the day.

Meteorology is the study of weather. This is an extremely important part of aviation. A pilot needs to know if there will be storms or high winds, which can cause turbulence, or unsteadiness, in an aircraft. If a pilot knows where bad weather is, they can avoid it if necessary. Pilots also need to be aware of rain, other precipitation, and conditions on the ground, too. Planes, especially smaller ones, can have trouble operating in dangerous weather conditions.

66 Please know I am quite aware of the hazards. I want to do it because I want to do it. Women must try to do things as men have tried. 99

—Amelia Earhart

After checking the weather, Meg finishes her preparations. "If I'm doing an intro flight," Meg says, "I make sure the full-motion flight simulator is ready to go." What is Meg talking about?

Flight simulators are an important technology in the field of aviation. A full-motion flight simulator is a machine that lets students practice their flying skills on the ground. The outside looks like a metal box set on a moveable platform. It's kind of like a giant, virtual reality video game you can sit in. The inside looks like a cockpit.

"The instructor can program the weather, the weight of the airplane, and fail the engine or any instrument by virtue of a keystroke," Meg explains. Because the machine can move on its platform, when you're sitting in the simulator, it really feels like you're flying a plane.

Other scientists, organizations, and businesses use simulators. For instance, the National Aeronautics and Space Administration (NASA) uses them so astronauts can practice working in the space shuttle and other spacecraft before a mission. The U.S. Air Force uses them to teach pilots how to fly expensive military planes. (You can read about one of them in chapter 4!) And shipping companies use them so their boat captains can practice sailing in all kinds of waters.

Cool Careers:
Air Traffic Controller

Sarina Gumbert is an air traffic controller in Florida. Air traffic controllers are people who read radar screens and keep track of airplanes in the air and on the ground. They communicate with pilots. It's an extremely important and stressful job. You need to be calm and focused and able to keep track of information.

In October 2014, Sarina noticed two planes in danger of colliding. She was able to tell one of the planes to move in time. Her actions earned her the Archie League Medal of Safety Award, the highest honor an air traffic controller can receive.

An air traffic control screen

When you first start to learn to fly, practicing in a simulator instead of in the air can have many advantages. For one, it's safer to practice skills you're just learning on the ground than it is to learn them in the air. "I can also hit the 'pause' button so the client and I can talk about the task at hand," Meg explains. Plus, you can practice a skill or maneuver over and over again. Can you think of any other advantages of using a flight simulator?

Teaching someone to fly takes a lot of time and preparation. Because of this, Meg tries not to have more than five students at a time.

Liftoff!

Flight simulators are training tools that give you the experience of flying without the danger. There are many video games that do the same thing, though usually not at the same level of quality as professional training simulators. You can take a look at what it's like to be inside a simulator with this video. What does it feel like? Can you forget that you've got both feet on the ground?

REAL Qantas 747 flight simulator 🔍

66 I have found that women are not only just as much interested as men are in flying, but apparently have less fear than the men have. 99

—Katherine Stinson,
the fourth woman in the United States
to obtain a pilot's certificate

A typical lesson between Meg and one of her students includes 10 to 20 minutes of briefing. This is talking about and demonstrating what they're about to do. Then they spend an hour either practicing in the simulator or flying in the air. Afterward, Meg and her student spend another 20 or 30 minutes discussing what they did. "Most people fly two to four times a week," says Meg.

You have to be at least 16 years old to fly solo in an airplane. Meg's students range in age from 16 to 60 and older.

Ask & Answer

Flight simulators are extremely valuable in aviation. Can you think of ways technology has helped other fields of science or industries? Research women who have been a part of technological innovations.

Most of Meg's students are men, but sometimes Meg gets to teach women. As the field of aviation grows, more and more young women are going into the field and learning to pilot.

Meg says she sometimes experiences sexism. This is when people believe that all boys should act a certain way and all girls should act a certain way, just because of their gender. Sexism is also when people form opinions about a person based on their gender. Some people see Meg wearing her brown leather flight jacket and assume it belongs to her father. They think that because she's a woman, Meg can't be a pilot.

Sexism is a form of discrimination. Discrimination is treating someone differently or harshly because of things such as their race, gender, or age. Thankfully, Meg has support. "My students, especially my male students, are quick to defend me when someone makes a sexist comment," she says.

66 Because of Amelia Earhart, we had more women available to fly in the 1940s to help get through World War II. And because of these women, women of my generation are able to look back and say, 'Hey, they did it. They even flew military airplanes, we can do it, too.' 99

—U.S. Air Force Colonel Eileen Collins,
first female space shuttle commander

photo credit: Pacific Aviation Museum

What advice does Meg have for young girls who might be interested in doing what she does? "If you want a career in aviation, focus on technical skills and subjects such as math and science," she says. "Although, don't count yourself out if the humanities [things such as writing, art, and history] are your strength."

Being a flight instructor takes patience and lots of energy. Meg loves teaching others how to fly.

"For most people, it is something they have wanted to do their whole lives," Meg says. "I help them achieve their dream. It is like teaching someone how to read, how to ride a bike, or how to swim. All three of these activities are life-altering, just like learning to fly."

CHAPTER 3

Taylor McConnell

Pilots are probably the most visible people in the field of aviation, but they are just a part of it. There are plenty of things that go on "behind the scenes" or on the ground. Many of the people who work in aviation don't work in a cockpit or at an airport. Taylor McConnell is one of them. She's a production support engineer for a company that makes airplanes.

Taylor was born March 20, 1993, in Columbus, Ohio. She is the middle child of three kids, with an older brother and a younger sister. Her father, Ryan, is an insurance examination data specialist. This is someone who analyzes information. Her mother, Stefanie, is a high school English and drama teacher.

Taylor has always had an interest in aviation and she dreams of being an astronaut someday. She describes herself as a curious child. "I always wanted to figure out how and why things worked," she says.

Thankfully, just as Orville and Wilber Wright's mother encouraged them, Taylor's parents supported and encouraged her curiosity. "They would give me things that broke so that I could try to fix them. And, if I was unsuccessful, I'd tear them apart and see if I could learn how they worked and fit together.

Ask & Answer

In the field of aviation, it seems pilots often get most of the attention. In what ways are people who work "behind the scenes" a vital part of aviation? Create a list of all the people you can think of who might help make sure an airplane's flight is safe.

Try This

Ask your parents for permission to use pliers and other tools to take apart a broken household item, such as a toaster or radio. Make sure to wear safety goggles and gloves. Be careful not to touch any circuit boards with your bare hands, because they can be toxic. Sort the parts into small containers. You can also recycle parts by creating art projects out of them.

"My parents always encouraged me to pursue my dreams. Regardless of what they were, my parents wanted me to work hard and fearlessly pursue my wildest ambitions," Taylor says.

Taylor's grandfather, Ron Harris, also encouraged her interest. Taylor calls her grandfather the "single biggest inspiration" in her life. She spent a lot of time with him when she was younger, and he often talked about his experiences as a technician in the Air Force.

While in the armed forces, Mr. Harris worked on a ballistic missiles program as well as on the Airborne Laser Lab project. Both of these projects were weapons systems.

Ask & Answer

Do you share a passion with one of your grandparents the way Taylor does?

Taylor says, "My most vivid memory of visiting my grandpa was when I was 12 and he explained, at length, how a ruby rod laser worked." A laser is a device that gathers, organizes, and focuses photons, or light particles, so they are going in the same direction.

Other times, Taylor's grandfather let her follow him and watch him fix things around the house. "He did his very best to answer every question I ever asked," Taylor says. When he was on the computer playing a flight simulator game, he'd let her take over and fly. Taylor's grandfather also took Taylor along when he flew model airplanes. When she got older, he'd let her fly them herself.

Taylor loved sports when she was younger. "On the playground in elementary school," she says, "I was one of about three girls who were allowed by the boys to play sports with them. They played slide-tackle soccer, and I thought it was so much more fun that way."

Lasers

The word laser is an acronym. It stands for Light Amplification by Stimulator Emission of Radiation. Taylor's grandfather taught her about the ruby rod lasers used in the military. But there are many different kinds of lasers. We use them every day in our lives. For example, lasers are used to play CDs and DVDs, to cut metal, for entertainment and sports, and for defense. They are also used in the medical field.

In the early 1980s, Dr. Patricia E. Bath (1942–) became the first African American women to receive a medical patent. Dr. Bath is an ophthalmologist, or someone who takes care of people's eyes. She invented a laser device called a laserphaco probe. It is used to remove cloudy spots, called cataracts, on eye lenses. This invention has helped millions of people see better.

Taylor also played competitive softball from the age of eight until age 16. "That consumed nearly every weekend I had during that time," she says. "I played catcher, and I loved every second of it."

Nose of the Battle of Britain Memorial Flight
Lancaster B1 bomber (PA474)

Taylor had two other passions. One was reading. "I mostly read fantasy books," Taylor says. "J.R.R. Tolkien and J.K. Rowling are my favorites. I could read the Harry Potter books a thousand times and still not get enough of them!"

Her other passion was music. She played the viola and still plays the trombone. Her family shared in this passion. "Everyone in my family (except my dad) either played an instrument or sang," Taylor reports.

Music is not the only family talent. It seems that an interest and talent in aviation are also legacies in Taylor's family. Not only was Taylor's grandfather in the Air Force, but her great-grandfather was in the "Mighty 8th Air Force." This was when military pilots were part of the Army Air Corps.

During World War II, her great-grandfather was a bomb toggle. This is the person who armed and dropped bombs from planes. He was also a nose gunner, the person who operated the gun at the front of the aircraft.

Nature vs. Nurture

Have you ever heard of the phrase "nature vs. nurture"? It's a concept that scientists have been debating for a long time. Do we inherit our behaviors and talents? Or do our personalities and skills come as a result of our environments?

The majority of researchers today believe that it's likely a mix of both. For example, a 2009 study at the University of California San Francisco showed that having perfect pitch, or the ability to detect the pitch of a musical tone without reference, tends to run in families. This falls into the nature category. However, it must be learned and practiced at a young age in order for it to show up. This puts the trait into the nurture column, too.

Think about Taylor. Was she was born with a passion for aviation or was her passion the result of being around other family members who were in the field? What do you think?

Rosie the Riveter

In the 1940s, many men, like Taylor's great-grandfather, went off to serve in World War II. The factories that built the airplanes and other military equipment needed workers, so they began hiring women. This was something new for the country. At the time, women were expected to be homemakers or teachers or secretaries.

Factory jobs, such as assembly line workers, were considered "men's work." The factories started an ad campaign to hire women. This campaign included images of a fictional woman called Rosie the Riveter. She was shown wearing a red bandana and flexing her muscles. Rosie's motto was "We Can Do It!"

Working in a factory was hard, physically demanding work. But the women showed that they were up to the challenge. Unfortunately, many of them lost their jobs after the soldiers came home and went back to work at the factories. But still, these women forever changed the way women were viewed in the workforce.

In 2000, the Rosie Riveter WWII Home Front National Historical Park was established in California.

> 66 You came out to California, put on your pants, and took your lunch pail to a man's job. This was the beginning of women feeling that they could be something more. 99
>
> **—Sybil Lewis,**
> a woman who helped build airplanes
> during World War II

Taylor's great-uncle got a degree in aeronautical engineering and worked for NASA for almost 40 years. While he was there, he got to work on the *Apollo 11* mission. This is the mission that landed men on the moon in 1969. Both Taylor's grandfather and great-uncle also got their private pilot's licenses after they left the military.

"It was really like I was born with this passion for aviation," Taylor say. "It just always made sense I'd go into it. There was never really a single, defining moment for me, it was just meant to be."

MAKING PLANS

When Taylor was in the sixth grade, she learned that many astronauts are engineers. So she set out to take this path. "This realization made perfect sense because engineers are builders. They create things or improve things," Taylor says, "and that is what I had always been interested in."

In high school, Taylor worked hard to improve her chances of being accepted at a top engineering school. She took every science and math class she possibly could.

Learning science and math is a good idea if you're interested in going into engineering or another field of science. Science classes, such as chemistry and physics, can teach critical thinking skills and the scientific principles that can be used to create new technologies. Engineering also often involves complicated mathematical calculations.

Toni Breese

Toni Breese is a licensed airframe and power plant mechanic, or airplane maintenance technician. Toni lives in Alaska. It's her job to inspect and perform daily maintenance on airplanes.

There aren't many women who do this job. It's estimated that only 2 percent of airplane mechanics are women! Toni learned her job by working as an apprentice. An apprentice is someone who trains or learns by working with an expert. It took Toni more than 30 months to train for her job.

Ask & Answer

When she was young, Taylor liked working with her hands and figuring out how things worked. Later, she found a job in which she did these things. Do you think you'll be able to get a job someday doing the things you love to do now?

After high school, Taylor decided to follow her great-uncle's lead and attend Purdue University in Indiana. Purdue has one of the top aerospace engineering programs in the United States. It also boasts the highest number of astronauts among its graduates.

People are often surprised to see a female mechanic. Sometimes, tourists even ask if they can take her picture! But Toni has a good sense of humor about it.

Toni also sees her gender as a plus. "As a woman in the industry, I tend to see things differently than the guys, which can be a great advantage. As a woman, I will see a completely different way to do something, repair, or approach a situation."

Female Astronauts

In 1978, in the first NASA class to include women (the first space shuttle class), only six out of the 35 astronauts were women. In the astronaut class of 2013, four out of the eight members were women!

Anne McClain, Jessica Meir, Christina Hammock Koch, and Nicole Aunapu Mann were chosen to train for the Mars mission. This mission is still at least 15 years away. Traveling to Mars is a major challenge. It will take up to nine months just to get there. And once they are on the red planet, astronauts will face many dangers, including giant dust storms and extremely frigid temperatures. They can't change their minds about coming home, either. They will be away from their families for at least two years.

Anne, a former military helicopter pilot, is looking forward to the chance to go to Mars someday. "With so much conflict in the world, space exploration can be a beacon of hope. No one cares about race or religion or nationality in space travel. We're all just part of Team Human," she says.

2013 Class of NASA astronaut candidates 🔍

2013 class of NASA astronaut candidates
photo credit: NASA

There are 23 Purdue graduates who have gone on to become astronauts. One of these is the man with the first footprint on the moon, Neil Armstrong. Another is the man to put the last footprint on the moon, Gene Cernan.

Taylor spent two years in the engineering program, but she discovered her heart wasn't in it. "It wasn't what I wanted," she says. "I was still interested in planes, I just didn't feel connected to my studies. I kept my eyes and ears open, and found my way to the aviation technology department and the aeronautical engineering technology department."

Ask & Answer

What would happen if everyone decided that the technology we have now is "good enough" and stopped trying to improve it?

Taylor soon switched her major to aeronautical engineering technology and was much happier. Switching meant she could work directly with aircraft, tearing down and working with engines. She knew immediately that she'd made the right decision.

While still in college, Taylor was able to do several internships. Internships are jobs, sometimes unpaid, where students or trainees can gain experience in the field. Through these experiences, Taylor learned how to read and interpret technical specifications and drawings. She also learned how planes are manufactured and how to monitor the process to make sure all the parts work the way they should.

At her last internship, Taylor got to walk around the factory where the planes were being built and watch the assembly process. She also developed a computer program that allowed the plant to input flight test numbers and then analyze those numbers. This allows testers to alter flight conditions to fix problems.

Jet Engines

How does a jet engine work? Jet engines use air and fire to create thrust, or forward motion. First, the engine uses a fan to suck air through the front of the engine. Next, a machine called a compressor uses fast-moving blades to squeeze the air. This raises the air's pressure. Fuel is sprayed on this compressed air and then lit on fire with a spark. This creates a burning gas that is pushed out of the back of the engine.

The pushing action at the back of the engine causes the front of the engine (and therefore the plane) to move forward. As that hot air is moving, it turns another set of blades called the turbine. The turbine spins, and since it's connected to the same bar as the compressor, the compressor spins, too.

Check out this site from NASA.

NASA kids jet engine 🔍

Turbojet engine being investigated in Cleveland, Ohio, 1946

photo credit: NASA

Taylor was fortunate to have incredible teachers in college. There are two who stand out the most for her—Mike Davis and Dr. Mary Johnson.

Professor Mike Davis taught Taylor's advanced aircraft power plants class, which focused on turbine engines.

Cool Careers:
Industrial Engineer

Dr. Mary Johnson, one of Taylor's professors at Purdue University, is an industrial engineer. An industrial engineer is someone who deals with complex processes or systems, such as machines and the people who use them, to make sure they are working efficiently together. In other words, they figure out how to make everything in a company run better. For example, an industrial engineer might figure out how to make sure the machines at a factory are safer for the workers or how to make the machines operate faster. They might even figure out how to shorten the lines at amusement parks! How do you think they might do this?

Ask & Answer

Do you have a teacher who has helped or inspired you? Write them a letter to thank them!

He was a former Air Force technician and used real-life stories to teach his students. "He also runs the part of the program that allows students to receive their airframe and power plant certification through the FAA," Taylor says.

This means students can become airplane mechanics, which was one of Taylor's goals, too. "Professor Davis is incredibly supportive of all the students and would do just about anything for you to make sure you make it through the program," she says.

Dr. Mary Johnson is an industrial engineer who teaches in the aviation technology department at Purdue. Taylor says, "She was my mentor during my time in the aeronautical engineering technology department." Mary gave Taylor much-needed encouragement and helped her find ways to fund her education. "She went out of her way to help me find paid internships and research opportunities," Taylor says.

Airplane Assembly

How many people work to assemble a commercial airliner? Check out this short, high-speed video to see a Boeing 777-200LR being put together.

Delta Boeing 777-200LR assembly 🔍

Mary does research on aircraft engine emissions. This means she studies the production and discharge of energy or gas waste from engines. Taylor was able work with her on a few projects.

"She's spent a good amount of time in the aerospace industry, so she passes on her invaluable knowledge on remaining successful in such a close-knit and competitive environment," Taylor says of her mentor.

> 66 I remember in third grade I asked my mom, 'How does an engine work?' So my mom bought me a book. 99

—Gwynne Shotwell,
president and chief operating officer of SpaceX

WORKING WITH PLANES

Taylor is just starting out in her aviation career. In the same way as she did when she was younger, she still dreams of working for NASA and going into space one day. For now, she's thrilled to work for an aircraft manufacturer. "I just really want to be near planes," Taylor says.

Taylor is a production support engineer. The job is also called a material review board engineer and liaison engineer. This is someone who makes sure all the parts of a machine are working properly. For Taylor, it means making sure all of the parts of an airplane are just as they should be.

Today, humans explore Mars through rovers, but, someday, Taylor might be part of a team to land on Mars!

photo credit: NASA

Cool Careers:
Aeronautical Analyst

Like Taylor McConnell, Sara McDale works in aviation, but not as a pilot. Sara is an aeronautical analyst. This is someone who collects and evaluates information, or data, to help pilots. For example, if there was an earthquake and an airport was damaged, pilots might need help finding safer places to land. To do this, aeronautical analysts use satellite images and special 3-D glasses to look at the terrain, or the earth's surface. Sara works at the National Geospatial-Intelligence Agency, a government agency that helps the military with missions.

Pilots need to know about large storms and other weather that can affect their flights.

photo credit: NASA

Taylor explains: "After the plane comes out of the factory, there are still a lot of parts that need to be installed and the whole plane needs to be painted. While all of this is happening, the plane sometimes gets damaged. Sometimes, we'll notice a part was made improperly."

Each day, Taylor goes to her office inside a hanger, the large building where aircraft are stored. She logs onto her computer to receive tags, which are reports from shop workers and mechanics about possible bad parts that they've seen while working on the aircraft.

Taylor uses the tags to locate the aircraft and investigate the questionable part. She then takes notes and photographs the damage.

It's Taylor's job to examine the part and determine a plan of action. She uses mathematical calculations, testing, and her skills as an FAA-certified mechanic to determine if a part is strong enough to use.

If a part can be repaired, Taylor writes a detailed, specific order for the mechanics to follow. If the part can't be repaired, Taylor orders a replacement. She must be very careful when examining the parts. She wants everyone who uses the plane to be safe! And it's especially interesting to her because she'd like to earn her own pilot's license, too, someday.

Ask & Answer

Taylor says she hasn't experienced much discrimination because of her gender while on the job. Do you think this would have been true 20 or 30 years ago?

Taylor loves interacting with aircraft every day. "I really love being able to walk out on the floor," she says. She also enjoys the challenge of solving different puzzles. "Every day is something new," Taylor says.

Because they're working on different things all the time, production support engineers needs to be open-minded. As in all technology fields, aviation changes frequently. The tools, materials, and manufacturing methods are constantly evolving. You must be willing to learn new things and be flexible.

You also need to have patience. Sometimes there is a reoccurring problem with a part and it takes a while to figure out what to do. You also need to be able to work with other people and communicate well.

Although sometimes people are surprised to hear what she does, Taylor hasn't experienced much sexism, either in college or on the job. Taylor says, "I firmly believe that if you approach individuals calmly and respectfully, gender is a non-issue."

Taylor has some advice for young women who are interested in going into aviation. "I encourage girls to fearlessly pursue it. There are a number of great schools that have programs involving aviation, whether it is in maintenance, management, or even to become a pilot.

"For many individuals in the industry, aviation is far more than just a job or career—it is their passion. This, in my opinion, is the single greatest thing about aviation. So read about it online, watch a documentary, find a book about planes or aviation at the library. There is so much you can do and learn about aviation on your own if you simply go looking for it."

66 Get involved, because those experiences will teach you so much and will also be invaluable if you decide to pursue it as a career. 99

—Taylor McConnell

CHAPTER 4
Kristin Wolfe

Kristin Wolfe has an important job. When other people need help in dangerous situations, she's ready. She doesn't wear a police badge, a fire helmet, or a stethoscope, but she does wear a uniform. Kristin is a pilot for the U.S. Air Force. She flies the F-22 Raptor. Her job is to train so she's always ready to fight enemy aircraft and keep people on the ground safe.

Kristin was born May 27, 1989, in California. Her dad, Jon, was a F-15C pilot in the U.S. Air Force. Her mom, Maria, mostly stayed home to care for Kristin and her younger brother and sister. Kristin describes herself as an Air Force "brat." A "military brat" is a friendly nickname some people use to describe kids whose parents are in the military and who move from base to base. A military base is a place where soldiers and their families live and where soldiers work and train.

The Air Force is a part of the country's military. The military, or armed forces, are the people who enforce security and protect the people of a country. The United States has five branches in its armed forces— the Army, Navy, Marines Corps, Coast Guard, and Air Force.

Each branch has a special job. The Army's soldiers fight land-based missions. The Navy's missions are at sea. The Coast Guard helps protect people on the ocean near the coastline.

Ask & Answer

Have you ever thought about becoming a soldier? Why do we need soldiers?

The Marines support missions on land and along the shores. And the Air Force is the branch that handles aerial warfare. Established in 1947, it is the youngest of the military branches. The U.S. Air Force is also the largest air force in the world.

Kristin and her brother and sister were homeschooled. This means that instead of going to a public or private school, they learned at home.

Esther McGowin Blake

On July 8, 1948, the U.S. Air Force officially opened its doors to women. The first woman to enlist was Esther McGowin Blake (1897–1979). She signed up on the first minute of the first hour of the first day! Esther was already in her late forties at the time. Her husband had died and her two sons were soldiers. She signed up so she could take over a desk job for a solider who could then be available to fight. It was her hope that this would help the war end faster. Esther earned the rank of staff sergeant and served until 1954.

Their mother taught them when Kristin was in grades two through six. "Initially, my parents decided to start homeschooling out of necessity due to military moves," Kristin says. "However, my siblings and I liked it so much that we continued for the next few years. I think the real success was due to my parents keeping us active in social activities as well, such as local homeschooling field trips, sports teams, church groups, and piano lessons."

Kristin feels that being homeschooled helped foster her independent, hands-on learning style. But she liked public school later, too.

She describes herself as "always very independent and sometimes pretty stubborn" as a child. She and her siblings like to play outdoors, participating in sports and building forts. Kristin always liked and did well in math and science, too.

For two summers, she attended an educational camp where she took classes on subjects such as physics.

Ask & Answer

Different people learn best in different ways. Kristin describes her learning style as hands-on. How do you learn best, by reading or listening to information? What might happen if schools only taught in one way?

In this class, the campers got to visit an amusement park and see how physics were applied in the design of roller coasters!

Because her father was in the Air Force and was a pilot, Kristin grew up around airplanes. But she never really thought about becoming a pilot herself.

Still, Kristin wasn't sure what she'd like to do when she grew up. "Growing up, I always knew I didn't want a typical desk job," she says.

Roller Coaster Physics

Kristin attended a camp where she got to explore the physics of roller coasters. Engineers need to have a good understanding of physics to design a roller coaster that is both fun and safe. You can try building your own virtual roller coaster here using the principles of physics.

Learner design roller coaster 🔍

photo credit: Alex Brogan

The WASPs

The U.S. military began using airplanes during World War I. But it wasn't until World War II that they began accepting female pilots. Though they weren't allowed to fly in combat missions, female aviators helped transport airplanes to military airfields, teach other pilots, and test aircraft.

This group was called Women Air Force Service Pilots, or WASPs. The WASPs were largely because of the efforts of Jacqueline "Jackie" Cochran (1906–1980) and Nancy Harkness Love (1914–1976).

Jackie Cochran was an American star pilot who set speed and altitude records. When the war began, she wrote to First Lady Eleanor Roosevelt and suggested that female pilots could be of use. She began training female pilots in Great Britain and eventually returned to the United States to start the Women's Flying Training Detachment.

Meanwhile, Nancy Love, a race and test pilot, created and became the commander of the Women's Auxiliary Ferrying Squadron. Many of her recruits came from Jackie's training group.

In 1943, the two groups merged to become WASP. Jackie was its first director, while Nancy was named executive of the ferrying operations. They helped prove that women were capable military pilots and valuable assets in the armed forces.

To read more about the WASP program, go to this website.

NPR original fly girls 🔍

TRAINING

Since she liked math and science, Kristin decided she'd study chemical engineering in college. A chemical engineer is someone who uses technology to produce products or energy using chemicals.

Kristin attended the University of Alabama. But after being in school for a couple of years, Kristin realized that chemical engineering wasn't the career path she wanted. She thought maybe she'd join the Marines instead. She asked her dad for his opinion. "He's always the one I go back to with questions and for advice," Kristin says.

Kristin's dad encouraged her to try the Air Force Reserve Officer Training Corp, or AFROTC, on campus. The AFROTC is a special program where college students go to learn and train to become officers in the Air Force. The Army, Navy, and Marines have ROTC programs as well. The Coast Guard does not have an ROTC program, although it does have an officer training program.

> 66 Don't think that you can't do something, because you can. You limit yourself if you say, 'I can't do it.' 99
>
> **—Evelyn Stewart Jackson,**
> a member of WASP

Ask & Answer

Do you ever go to your parents for advice the way Kristin does?

Since she was already close to finishing her degree, Kristin decided to complete her studies in chemical engineering. But she took her dad's advice and joined the AFROTC as well.

Kristin did very well in the AFROTC program. She studied hard and got excellent grades. And her experiences as a high school soccer player and cross-country runner helped her do well in the physical training section of the program.

After college, Kristin joined the Air Force. "After growing up in a military family, I realized I was drawn to the challenges and the disciplined environment," Kristin says.

She also liked the idea of getting to move often. Military families such as Kristin's have to move a lot. Because she'd done it as a child, she thought it would be interesting to live in many different places as a grownup, too.

Soon after joining the Air Force, Kristin started training to become a pilot. The first step was attending initial flight training, which at the time was called initial flight screening, in Colorado. It's an academic program where soldiers learn everything they need to know about flying.

Some of the people there had never flown. Others already knew how to fly. But being a military pilot is different from being a private or commercial pilot. You have to learn all of the military procedures and you have to learn how to fight.

Call Signs

Fighter pilots have nicknames, or call signs. It's a long-standing military tradition. Sometimes, call signs are based on someone's personality, but often they're related to the person's last name. For example, Kristin's call sign is Beo. It's inspired by her last name, Wolfe. There is a famous Old English poem called "Beowulf." You don't get to pick your call sign, instead, your peers choose it for you. See if you and a group of your friends can come up with call signs for each other!

The initial flight training program is very competitive. Not everybody is allowed to participate. Just as in the rest of the field of aviation and the military, men outnumber women. Each initial flight training class has about 25 students. Out of the 25, an average of only one or two students are women.

The program is very demanding. For example, students are asked to stand up and describe how they would handle an emergency without any preparation. "The entire process is very challenging, yet very rewarding at the same time," Kristin says.

Colleen Nevius

Even though Kristin hasn't personally experienced gender discrimination, many of the women in the military who came before her did. This includes retired Captain Colleen Nevius. She was the first woman to graduate from the U.S. naval test pilot school. The Navy didn't allow women on combat ships until 1978. And once they were allowed on the ships, Colleen says she and her fellow female pilots had to work even harder to prove themselves. "I just felt this pressure that if I was out, they were not going to give other women the chance," Colleen said.

"I have always been driven to do well at any task, so oftentimes that was motivation enough to excel. After long hours or difficult days, being offered the opportunity to be in a hands-on career where I wasn't behind a desk most days was also motivation," Kristen adds.

66 Flying is a great equalizer. The plane doesn't know or care about your gender as a pilot, nor do the ground troops who need your support. 99

—Lt. Col. Christine Mau,
the first female to fly the F-35 Lightning II jet

Sometimes male soldiers acted as if women couldn't handle flying. Colleen and other female pilots simply showed they could do it. "You gained your credibility with your time in the cockpits . . . . The aircraft never ever knew the difference. It was always kind of entertaining to take off your helmet in the fuel pits and they [men] were like, 'But who's flying?'"

You can hear about Colleen's experiences here.

NAVAIR first female naval test pilot 🔍

Ask & Answer

Only a few of Kristin's classmates in the pilot training program were women. How do you think it would feel to be surrounded by people of the opposite gender? Do you think you would have a hard time competing?

A couple of generations ago, many people believed women weren't as physically and emotionally strong as men. They felt women shouldn't be soldiers or airmen because they wouldn't be able to handle the job. You might be surprised to hear that some people still feel this way. But, today, the military is working to make sure men and women are treated the same.

Kristin says she's never personally experienced sexism. "The military is extremely good about providing an equal environment for everyone," she says. "I've never heard of or experienced any discrimination between males and females in the workplace."

After going through the initial training, Kristin and her classmates went to a base in Texas. There, they took more classes and continued learning how to pilot military airplanes. They spent a great deal of time in flight simulators.

Cool Careers:
Aerial Firefighter

When a wildfire breaks out, it can be difficult — and dangerous — to drive a fire truck into the fire to help. This is when aerial firefighters using helicopters can fly in to lend a hand. Helicopters and airplanes equipped with special tanks or buckets can scoop water out of a lake or river and then drop it from the air. They are used frequently in drought-stricken California. The California Department of Forestry and Fire Protection, or Cal Fire for short, is the state organization in charge.

In 2015, Desiree Horton became the first woman to be a full-time member of the Cal Fire team. It's her dream job. Desiree got her pilot's license when she was 21. She flew for a news station, reporting the news and traffic, but always had a passion to be an aerial firefighter. The job can be dangerous. In addition to dropping water on fires, these pilots also transport firefighters to the frontline of a wildfire. High winds, fire, heat, and smoke are constant challenges.

"I don't think of it any differently, male or female, because I do the same job the guys do," Desiree says.

You can see a news report about Desiree here.

first woman CAL FIRE pilot video 🔍

Ask & Answer

Some people think women should have limited roles in the military. For example, they think women shouldn't be in combat. What do you think? Why?

From start to finish, Kristin's training took about two years. The only thing left for Kristin to do was to decide if she wanted to become a bomber pilot or a fighter pilot.

Throughout her training, Kristin got to meet and talk with other pilots. Because she felt she'd fit in best with the fighter pilot community, and because she felt that the job of fighter pilot would suit her best, she chose to become a fighter pilot.

> 66 If you can't see any opportunities where you are now, don't waste your time criticizing the darkness . . .. Light a candle to find your way out. 99

—Arlene Feldman,
pilot and first female regional administrator
for the FAA

FLYING THE RAPTOR

The airplane Kristin flies is called the F-22 Raptor. It's a stealth airplane. The word *stealth* means "the act of moving or behaving in a secret or quiet way." Most aircraft can be tracked by radar on the ground or in the air. Stealth planes are designed so that they aren't easily detected by radar.

To understand how stealth technology works, you have to first understand how radar works. Radar sends out radio waves. The waves travel outward until they "hit" an object. Then they bounce back to the radar. Based on how long it takes for this to happen, the radar can figure out how far away an object is.

F-22 Raptors from Elmendorf Air Force Base fly over Alaska.

photo credit: U.S. Air Force

Radar can also figure out the speed and size of an object. We use radar all the time. For example, meteorologists, the people who study weather, use radar to track storms. Police officers use radar to see how fast cars are going.

Stealth airplanes are designed to make it harder for the radar's radio waves to "hit" them. Flat surfaces and sharp angles help to hide the planes. Stealth planes are also covered with special materials that absorb the radio waves.

Jackie Cochran

How you ever been watching a fast plane and heard a boom? That sound is the result of the plane breaking the sound barrier. This means it's traveling faster than the speed of sound. The sound you hear is called a sonic boom. It's caused by sound waves, which can't get out of the way fast enough. The sound waves pile up and are forced together all at once. Here's an interesting fact—the crack of a whip is a tiny sonic boom!

Jackie Cochran was the first female pilot to break the sound barrier. Jackie was born in Florida and grew up in poverty. She became a beautician and dreamed of owning her own makeup company.

Here's a simple way to see how much harder it is for radar to find a stealth plane. First, have a friend hold a piece of paper perpendicular in relationship to the floor. Have the friend stand at one end of a dark hall or room and then turn off the lights. Move a flashlight around until you find the piece of paper.

Next, have your friend turn the piece of paper so that it's parallel to the floor. Which is harder to find, the flat surface of the piece of paper or the edge of the piece of paper?

In the 1930s, after someone suggested flying would be the best way to meet with clients, she took up flying and quickly earned her pilot's license. She began to enter races and she set flight records. She was nicknamed "The Speed Queen."

After World War II (see the WASPs on page 76), she began flying jets. Piloting a jet called the F-86 Sabre, Jackie went faster than the speed of sound on May 18, 1953, in California.

Ask & Answer

Military pilots rely on their airplane's onboard technology, such as the radar, to keep them safe and to track and fight the enemy. What kind of technology do you rely on in your daily life?

The F-22 Raptor is a very fast airplane. It's capable of something called supercruise, which means it can travel at airspeeds greater that 1.5 Mach without using afterburners. Afterburners on jet planes give them a burst of thrust.

In simpler terms, the Raptor can go more than 1,100 miles per hour, or 1.5 times faster than the speed of sound! The Raptor is also highly maneuverable. This means it's easy to move and direct while in the air.

With the latest technology onboard, the Raptor is one of the Air Force's most advanced planes. Multiple computer screens allow the pilot to manage the aircraft easily, as well as see, track, and attack the enemy before the enemy can see the Raptor. It can engage in air-to-air combat as well as air-to-ground combat. This means it can fight enemy planes in the air and enemy troops on the ground.

As you can imagine, learning to fly the F-22 is quite challenging. After her initial training sessions, Kristin spent another eight months learning to fly the Raptor. First, she had to put in many, many hours practicing in the flight simulator.

She got to actually fly the Raptor about two months into training. And since the Raptor has only one seat, there was no instructor next to her to help the first time she flew it! But that doesn't mean she was alone.

Civil Air Patrol

One of the organizations Kristin recommends to people interested in aviation is the Civil Air Patrol (CAP). CAP is a nationwide group made up of civilian (non-military) volunteers who help the Air Force. The group provides three main services. It helps in emergencies, such as search and rescue missions, and helps in disaster relief operations. It also helps to educate young people and the general public about flying. If you are between the ages of 12 and 18, you can become a CAP cadet, a trainee.

Civil Air Patrol

"The first time you go fly it, you have an instructor right next to you in a chase plane," Kristin explained in a 2015 *Aviation for Women* article. A chase plane is a plane that flies alongside another plane to observe it. Chase planes are also used during emergencies to help guide pilots.

"It's pretty nerve-wracking knowing that you're holding a 150-million-dollar airplane in your hands and you better not mess that up," Kristin said about flying the Raptor in the article. "But they train you so well that your training takes over and when you come in to land for the first time . . . you're able to land just perfectly from doing the simulator rides."

In Action

Would you like to see the F-22 Raptor in action? You can see just how maneuverable the fighter plane is in these two videos. (Kristin isn't the pilot in either of these videos.) Keep an eye out for the vertical takeoff!

F-22 Raptor maneuverability demonstration 🔍

F-22 Raptor vertical takeoff 🔍

> **66** The aircraft does not know or understand gender. It only knows the difference in a true pilot and one who was perhaps not meant to fly. **99**

—Capt. Jennifer Kaye,
Air National Guard

Kristin's job is to train so she's always ready to fight if she's needed in battle. Her daily schedule varies. If she's practicing flying one day, she attends a briefing a couple of hours ahead of her takeoff time. Then, she puts on her flight gear and goes out to fly for about an hour.

"Afterward, we have a debrief, where we talk about all the things we did right and wrong and how we can do better the next time we go fly," Kristin says.

F-22 Raptor in vertical takeoff
photo credit: U.S. Air Force

If Kristin isn't scheduled to fly, she does other things. "Everyone has specific jobs they're assigned in the squadron, so if I'm not scheduled to fly, I'll be doing another job or studying for flying," she says. Kristin is always striving to improve. She holds herself to a very high standard. But, she says, most fighter pilots are like that.

"[They] tend to be hard workers and go-getters who like to get the job done well," Kristin says. "One of the great things about my job is the variety of people I work with. There's always an assortment of different ages, hometowns, college majors, prior flying experience, etc. [And] no two work days or flights are ever the same."

Kristin is currently a captain in the U.S. Air Force. All military branches have a ranking system that shows a chain of command, or who's in charge. An airman's rank is based on a number of things, such as experience, skill, and training.

Ask & Answer

Do you think different personality types are best suited for different jobs? Why or why not? What kind of personality do you have? Do you think it will make you better at doing specific things?

Kristin in front of an F-22 Raptor

Kristin made a 10-year commitment to the Air Force and she has another six years of service before deciding what she'd like to do next. "My parents are very proud of my military service as a pilot, especially my father," Kristin says.

When asked about her advice for girls who are interested in going into aviation, Kristin says, "Use any outlet you can to explore aviation, whether it be a local flying club, Civil Air Patrol, or even just reading aviation-related articles or books."

66 Whether it becomes a hobby or you make a career of it, I think you'll find aviation an extremely rewarding experience. 99

—Kristin Wolfe

Ninth Century BCE

- The Greek myth about Daedalus and his son, Icarus, is one of the first stories of humans in flight.

Fifteenth Century CE

- Leonardo da Vinci (1452–1519), an artist and inventor, watches birds and sketches ornithopters. He improves our understanding of human flight.

Eighteenth Century

- Sir George Cayley (1773–1857) begins experimenting with gliders.

Nineteenth Century

- Otto Lilienthal (1848–1896) improves the glider and is called "the world's first true aviator."

- Airships are popular but prove to be fairly dangerous.

1903

- Orville and Wilber Wright build and fly the first airplane. Katharine Wright, their younger sister, is often called the "Third Wright Brother" for her contributions in helping her brothers with the feat.

1910

- A French woman named Elise Raymonde de Laroche (1882–1919) becomes the first female pilot.

1911

- Harriet Quimby (1875–1912) becomes the first American woman to earn her pilot's license. She is the first woman to fly at night and the first woman to fly solo across the English Channel.

1921

- Bessie Coleman (1892–1926) becomes the first African American woman to earn a pilot's license.

1929

- The Ninety-Nines, the first organization of female pilots, is formed.

1934

- Helen Richey (1909–1947) becomes the first American female pilot to be hired by a commercial airline. After facing much discrimination, she leaves 10 months later and returns to flying at air shows and competitions.

Timeline

1937

- Amelia Earhart, arguably the most famous female pilot ever and the first person to fly solo across the Atlantic Ocean, disappears while attempting to become the first woman to fly around the world.

1940s

- During World War II, women take jobs at factories to build military airplanes and bombs to aid in the war effort. They are part of the "Rosie the Riveter" campaign.

- Jacqueline "Jackie" Cochran (1906–1980) and Nancy Love (1914–1976) help form the Women Air Force Service Pilots, or WASPs.

1953

- Jackie Cochran becomes the first woman to break the sound barrier.

1964

- American pilot Geraldine "Jerrie" Mock (1925–2014) is the first woman to accomplish what Amelia Earhart set out to do—fly around the world.

1973

- Emily Howell Warner (1939–) becomes the first female captain of a U.S. commercial airline.

1986

- Jeana Yeager (1952–) and her co-pilot, Dick Rutan, become the first aviators to fly around the globe without stopping to refuel.

1999

- Eileen Collins (1956–), a former test pilot in the Air Force, is the first female space shuttle commander.

2007

- Created by the mother-daughter team Nancy and Deanie Parrish, the "Fly Girls of WWII" WASP exhibit goes on display at the Women's Memorial in Washington, D.C. The exhibit is on permanent display at the Kalamazoo Air Zoo in Michigan.

2012

- President Barack Obama issues the Congressional Gold Medal to the members of the WASPs for their contributions.

Ask & Answer

Chapter 1

- Why do you think early aviators kept trying to fly even though their work was often dangerous?

- The early planes were made of wood. Today, we usually use a metal called aluminum. Why do you think that is?

- Which would make you want to try something new and challenging: having someone tell you that you *can* do something or someone telling you that you *can't* do something? Why?

Chapter 2

- Has anyone ever told you that you can't do something just because you're a girl or a boy or because you have a physical limitation? How did that make you feel?

- It can take a long time to become a pilot. Many people give up along the way. Have you ever done anything that took a long time to achieve? What made you stick with it?

- Meg thought getting her commercial pilot's license would give her more authority when she wrote about aviation. Do you think people who write about things should be able do them? Can you be an expert on something without experiencing it?

- What traits do you think a good teacher has? Do you think you'd be a good teacher?

- Flight simulators are extremely valuable in aviation. Can you think of ways technology has helped other fields of science or industries? Research women who have been a part of technological innovations.

Chapter 3

- In the field of aviation, it seems pilots often get most of the attention. In what ways are people who work "behind the scenes" a vital part of aviation? Create a list of all the people you can think of who might help make sure an airplane's flight is safe.

Ask & Answer

- Do you share a passion with one of your grandparents the way Taylor does?

- When she was young, Taylor liked working with her hands and figuring out how things worked. Later, she found a job in which she did these things. Do you think you'll be able to get a job someday doing the things you love to do now?

- What would happen if everyone decided that the technology we have now is "good enough" and stopped trying to improve it?

- Do you have a teacher who has helped or inspired you? Write them a letter to thank them!

- Taylor says she hasn't experienced much discrimination because of her gender while on the job. Do you think this would have been true 20 or 30 years ago?

Chapter 4

- Have you ever thought about becoming a soldier? Why do we need soldiers?

- Different people learn best in different ways. Kristin describes her learning style as hands-on. How do you learn best, by reading or listening to information? What might happen if schools only taught in one way?

- Do you ever go to your parents for advice the way Kristin does?

- Only a few of Kristin's classmates in the pilot training program were women. How do you think it would feel to be surrounded by people of the opposite gender? Do you think you would have a hard time competing?

- Some people think women should have limited roles in the military. For example, they think women shouldn't be in combat. What do you think? Why?

- Military pilots rely on their airplane's onboard technology, such as the radar, to keep them safe and to track and fight the enemy. What kind of technology do you rely on in your daily life?

- Do you think different personality types are best suited for different jobs? Why or why not? What kind of personality do you have? Do you think it will make you better at doing specific things?

acronym: a word formed from initials.

aerial: something that is in or has to do with the air.

aeronautical engineer: someone who figures out how to make all the parts of an aircraft work together.

aeronautics: the science of flight.

aerospace: an industry concerned with designing and building aircraft and other flying things such as missiles and spacecraft.

afterburner: the part of a jet engine that provides an increase in thrust.

aircraft: a vehicle that uses air or buoyancy to fly.

airfoil: the shape of a wing or any surface that is designed to lift or control an aircraft, including wings, rudders, and propellers.

airship: aircraft with an engine and rudder for steering.

air show: an exhibition of aircraft or aviation skills.

altitude: the height of an object above sea level.

aluminum: a lightweight but strong, silvery-gray metal.

apprentice: a person who learns a job or skill by working for someone who is good at it.

aviation: any activity that has to do with flying.

aviator: someone who operates an aircraft, especially an airplane.

aviatrix: a female aviator.

ballistics: the science that studies the movement of objects that are shot through the air.

base: a place where soldiers live with their families and train.

bi-wing: with two sets of wings.

biplane: aircraft that has two sets of wings, one above the other, double-decker style.

blimp: an airship with no rigid framework.

blockade: to block off.

brief: a meeting to discuss an event.

buoyancy: the force that makes something able to float, either in the air or in the water.

bush pilot: a pilot who flies in remote and inhospitable areas of the world.

call sign: the nickname your peers give you when you're a fighter pilot.

cambered wing: an unevenly curved wing.

cabin crew: everyone who works inside an airplane, including the captain or pilot, co-captain or co-pilot, navigator, and flight attendants.

cataract: a clouding of the eye's natural lens.

certified flight instructor: someone who teaches someone how to operate an airplane and prepare for the pilot's license test.

chemical engineering: using technology to produce products or energy using chemicals.

codex: a notebook or collection of pages, kind of like a journal.

combat: war, or fighting between armed forces.

commercial: operating as a business to earn money.

commercial pilot's license: a license given to pilots who are trained to fly commercial planes. Commercial planes are ones that transport public passengers.

culture: a group of people and their beliefs and way of life.

current: the steady flow of water or air in one direction.

debrief: to question someone about an experience.

dense: how tightly packed something is.

dirigible: airships with engines and rudders for steering. There are two types: zeppelins (which have rigid frames) and blimps (which have no rigid, internal structures).

discipline: control gained through training and hard work.

discrimination: when people are treated differently or more harshly because of things such as race, gender, or age.

drone: an unmanned aerial vehicle.

engineer: someone who designs, builds, or maintains things (especially machines, engines).

FAA: Federal Aviation Administration, the U.S. governmental organization that regulates and oversees everything having to do with aviation in America.

flight engineer: the member of the flight crew of an airplane responsible for its mechanical operation.

Flyer: the name of Orville and Wilber Wright's airplane that took the first successful flight.

glider: aircraft without an engine that floats (or glides) on air currents after being launched.

goods: things to use or sell.

ground instructor: someone who teaches people what they need to know to pass the written part of their pilot's test.

hanger: a large building where aircraft are kept.

homeschool: to be educated at home instead of at an institution.

hot air balloon: an aircraft made of an inflatable, fabric sack and basket. Heated air lifts it off the ground.

hydrogen gas: a colorless, odorless, and flammable gas that is lighter than air.

inhospitable: an area characterized by harsh conditions that are difficult to live in.

internship: a job, often unpaid, where students or trainees can gain experience in their field.

jetliner: an airplane that is powered by one or more jet engines. It can hold a large number of people.

journalist: someone who writes for a newspaper or magazine or prepares news for broadcast.

labyrinth: a maze.

laser: a device that gathers, organizes, and focuses photons (light particles).

Mach: the number indicating the ratio of the speed of an object to the speed of sound, especially as the object travels through air.

maneuverable: able to be easily manipulated and moved.

meteorology: the study of weather.

modification: a change.

motivation: a reason to do something.

mythology: a collection of traditional stories, either truthful or overly elaborated, that are often focused on historical events. Myths express the beliefs and values of a group of people.

navigator: the person who is in charge of planning and keeping track of an airplane's flight route.

ornithopter: an aircraft that flies with the use of wings that are flapped by mechanical means.

parallel: when two lines going in the same direction never touch, such as an equal (=) sign.

perpendicular: when an object forms a right angle with another object.

physics: the study of physical forces, including matter, energy, and motion, and how these forces interact with each other.

pilot: someone who flies an aircraft, especially an airplane.

pitch: an airplane's ability to move up (climb) or down (dive).

pressure: the force that pushes on an object.

Glossary

production support engineer: an engineer who resolves problems in a plane before it's sold.

propeller: a piece of equipment with blades that spin, used for moving a ship or aircraft.

protagonist: one of the main characters in a book, movie, or other fictional media.

radar: a device that detects objects by bouncing radio waves off them and measuring how long it takes for the waves to return.

radio wave: an electromagnetic wave used to send out radio signals through the air.

roll: an airplane's wings' ability to tip from side to side.

rudder: a fin-like device used to steer a vehicle through water or air.

sexism: the belief that you should look or behave a certain way because of your gender.

simulator: a machine with a set of controls designed to provide a realistic imitation of the operation of a vehicle, aircraft, or other complex system. Used for training purposes.

solo: alone or doing something alone.

sonic boom: the sound created by an object traveling through the air faster than the speed of sound.

stealth technology: designs that aircraft use to "hide" from enemy radar.

steam engine: an engine that burns wood or coal to heat water and create steam.

supercruise: the ability of a plane to travel at airspeeds faster than 1.5 Mach (1.5 times the speed of sound) without using afterburners.

technology: the scientific or mechanical tools, methods, and systems used to solve a problem or do work.

thrust: a force that pushes an object forward.

toxic: poisonous.

troops: large groups of soldiers.

turbine: a machine with blades turned by the force of water, air, or steam.

turbulence: strong winds or the unsteadiness they cause in an aircraft.

vessel: a ship or large boat.

World War II: a world war fought from 1939 to 1945.

yaw: an airplane's ability to move either left or right.

zeppelin: an airship that has a rigid, internal frame.

Resources

Books and Articles

- *First to Fly: How Wilbur and Orville Wright Invented the Airplane.* Busby, Peter. Madison Press Books, New York, 2002.
- *Women Aviators: 26 Stories of Pioneer Flights, Daring Missions, and Record-Setting Journeys (Women of Action).* Bush Gibson, Karen. Chicago Review Press, 2013.
- *Air and Space: The National Air and Space Museum Story of Flight.* Chaikin, Andrew. The Smithsonian Institution in association with Little, Brown and Co., New York, 1997.
- *"Congratulations Meg!"* General Aviation News, July 25, 2013.
- *Flying Machines (Eyewitness Books).* Nahum, Andrew. Alfred A. Knopf Inc., New York, 1990.
- *Aerospace Engineering and the Principles of Flight.* Rooney, Anne. Crabtree Publishing, New York, 2012.
- *"Zero to F-22: Kristin Wolfe masters the Raptor."* Stanton, Beth E. *Aviation for Women*, November/December 2015.

Websites and Museums

- 99s Museum of Women Pilots: *ninety-nines.org/99s-museum-of-women-pilots.htm*
- Alaska Dispatch News: *adn.com/article/where-are-all-women-alaska-aviation*
- FAA: *faa.gov*
- Intrepid Sea, Air & Space Museum: *intrepidmuseum.org*
- Lockheed Martin/Rosie the Riveter: *lockheedmartin.com/us/100years/stories/rosie-the-riveter.html*
- Master Instructor: *masterinstructors.org*
- Smithsonian National Air and Space Museum: *airandspace.si.edu*
- National Museum of the US Air Force: *nationalmuseum.af.mil*
- Teaching Women to Fly: *teachingwomentofly.com*

Resources

Websites and Museums (cont.)

- University of California San Fransisco: *ucsf.edu/news/2009/07/4263/perfect-pitch-study-offers-window-influences-nature-and-nurture*
- Wiggle Wings: *wigglywings.weebly.com*
- Women in Aviation: *wai.org*
- Wright Brothers Aeroplane Company: *wright-brothers.org*

QR Code Glossary

- Page 6: airandspace.si.edu/exhibitions/codex
- Page 8: archive.org/details/SF145
- Page 10: paperairplaneshq.com/paper-airplanes.html
- Page 13: nasa.gov/multimedia/imagegallery/image_feature_976.html
- Page 15: wai.org/resources/history.cfm
- Page 19: pbs.org/wgbh/americanexperience/features/timeline/earhart
- Page 29: wigglywings.weebly.com
- Page 33: youtube.com/watch?v = 3g1ccsdMM0g
- Page 35: jukebox.uaf.edu/site7/p/2494
- Page 42: youtube.com/watch?v = L8JUWUKXV08
- Page 58: nasa.gov/content/2013-class-of-nasa-astronaut-candidates
- Page 61: grc.nasa.gov/WWW/k-12/UEET/StudentSite/engines.html
- Page 64: youtube.com/watch?v = CZL5VFKb5Vo
- Page 75: learner.org/interactives/parkphysics/coaster
- Page 76: npr.org/2010/03/09/123773525/female-wwii-pilots-the-original-fly-girls
- Page 81: youtube.com/watch?v = 2PaD0_baoE0
- Page 83: youtube.com/watch?v = XRIcUyFcKHI
- Page 89: members.gocivilairpatrol.com/index.cfm
- Page 90: youtube.com/watch?v = ELo1NRMHuR8
- Page 90: youtube.com/watch?v = totzfPN4hWQ

Index

16 (0)

19 95